Aunt Jessica

ELLA WALKER

CONTENTS

CHAPTER 1

New Beginnings

I remember the crisp, cool weather day that I met my first foster parents. I was excited, nervous, and a little scared. To tell the truth, more scared than anything.

It was the first time that I would be living with someone that is not a part of my family.

My new foster parents met me at the front door and welcomed me to their home.

As I entered their living room, there were two dogs sitting on the chairs.

I was told that I would meet the other children this afternoon when they came home from school.

My new foster mother explained that her and her husband have two children of their own, and two foster children.

My foster mother, Mrs. Davis showed me to a bedroom that I would share with their daughter, Sara.

The foster dad, Mr. Davis, was a quiet man, he did not talk much.

After I put my bag on my new bed, Mrs. Davis invited me to come to the kitchen for a snack.

I remember asking questions in my head like what do I call my foster parents? Mr. and Mrs. Davis or Mom and Dad?

I wondered would I get along with the other children in the family?

My foster mother, Mrs. Davis told me that she would take me to register at my new school tomorrow.

Mrs. Davis asked me a lot of questions about my life. She told me that my caseworker had told them about my family and how I ended up becoming a foster child.

I remember thinking —how dare the social worker tell this total stranger about my life? I was very embarrassed and hurt.

Mrs. Davis was kind and gentle. She explained that the reason that she and her husband decided to become foster parents was to be able to offer a safe home for children who needed it.

I was very embarrassed about my life, but began to relax a little with the kindness that she showed me.

At around 3:30 pm. the other kids came home. I met their children, two girls, one in Jr. High school and one in High School. Then I met the two foster kids, who were sisters.

I remember thinking that at least I am not the only outsider here. Then I thought about the fact that I was all alone, at least the other two foster kids had each other, since they were sisters.

I thought about my own sister, but she was very far away, already married with kids of her own in another state.

At 6PM that night, we had supper. Mr. Davis was present. He led the Prayer of Thanksgiving.

This was a new experience for me. I had never sat down at a table for a meal with a Mom, Dad and kids like a real family. Deep in my heart, I always wanted a real family that I could call my own.

The first night that I shared a bedroom with their daughter Sara was interesting.

Sara was happy to have someone close to her age to talk to. I was so nervous that night, I was sure that I would not sleep a wink .but I did.

Before I knew it, I had to get ready for my first day ay my new school. I remember being so scared, it was a big school. I was grateful that my foster sister, Sara went there too. We would meet in the lunchroom every day.

Sara and I became good friends. The big sister that was in high school, her name was Nedra, would look out for me also. I remember the time that I had problems at school, when the kids found out that I was in a foster home,and were mean to me. Nedra and her friends showed up to defend me.

The kids left me alone after that, because they knew that I had a protector.

I really began to like school. Every Friday night, there was a dance in the Gym. Teachers and parents were chaperones. I was always nervous; I wanted to get out on the floor and dance.

I was way too shy, so I just stood by the wall with the other girls.

The teachers were good to me. I was way behind in school, so the teachers were patient with me.

I really liked English class. The teacher was very cool. He wore Bell Bottom Jeans. He had a rule-if the whole class finished all of the assigned work, then we could read quietly till the end of class.

At home .there was a rule that all of us kids would come to the dinner table to do our homework. We would end up helping each other. Of course, Nedra did her homework in her bedroom.

I began to accept this home as my own.

CHAPTER 2

Home

My foster sister, Nedra started sharing clothes her clothes with me. We were close to the same size.

I used to wonder what it would have been like to share clothes with my real sister. At night when Sara and I would be in our bedroom. We would talk about all kinds of things and share some our deep, dark secrets.

I know that each of us kept some secrets to ourselves. We would talk about cute boys, ect.

I used to watch Sara walk to her religious class on Sunday, while I stayed with the family. At times Sara would share her beliefs and doubts about God.

I always felt at peace at Mass. Our Mass was called a guitar mass. Music always touches my heart.

I looked forward to going to church with the whole family. Every Sunday when Mass was over, I got to shake the Priest's hand.

There were special days in our home, like birthdays and all the holidays.

Sometimes Sara and I would argue like sisters over chore.

On Saturdays, everyone except Mr. Davis would gather to clean the house. We all had assigned chores, according to age.

I loved walking the dogs, cleaning windows and vacuuming. I would daydream that I was cleaning my own home.

I don't remember the first time that I called Mrs. Davis – Mom. I was so scared. But I wanted her to be my Mom. She did the things that I thought that a mother should do.

We always had good food and plenty of it. No one went hungry in her house. Every Friday, we ate fish instead of meat. It was a Catholic thing. I love the taste of fish.

My foster Dad kind of left the parenting up to his wife. They had a traditional marriage. Mrs. Davis stayed home and Mr. Davis worked full time.

Mrs. Davis would take me and Sara shopping trips for food and clothes. We always stopped for ice cream on the way home for a treat.

The other girls did not go with us but stayed at home with Nedra to watch them. Nedra would shop none her own or with her girlfriends. The two foster sisters had their own day to shop with Mrs. Davis.

I remember when it was Christmas, I was so excited. I had never had a real Christmas, with a sparkly tree and Christmas music. We took naps during the day, because we had to go to Midnight Mass that night.

The church was so quiet and peaceful.

I remember looking up at the statue of Jesus. I told him-in my head-Thank-You for loving me. I could feel the silent tears running down my cheeks. I figured that he must Love a lot. He gave me a home in the truest sense of the word.

I did not realize it then but Mrs. Davis-Mom was teaching Sara and I housekeeping skills that we would need when we became adults.

Mom made our shopping trips fun and taught us how to budget our money for food and clothes.

There were times when I just wanted to hug this woman, because I knew that she cared about me and would keep me safe. She never judged me, even when she knew about my rotten background.

I never did hug her first, but I did hug her back, if she hugged me.

Every day I was reminded of the fact that she was not my real mom. No matter how much I wanted her for my mom. All I had to do is look at her kids, who strongly favored her to remind me of the fact that there would always be a certain amount of distance between us.

I remember parent teacher conference day, at school. Mrs. Davis never missed any of them. I was not a good student, my grades were poor, but she knew that I did my best. Every night she saw me doi8ng my homework with the other kids. She would always encourage me.

When I did do well .I couldn't wait to show her. I wanted her approval so much.

I remember the snow blizzards, and how hard it was to walk to school. I remember my bones aching from the cold weather. I guess that I was like my PawPaw-[Grandpa]. He could always tell what the weather was going to be. In cold weather his body would just plain old hurt.

I remember in my times that I was alone. I would like to draw. I would draw houses. I would dream about nice homes that I would like to have with big bay windows to let the sunshine in. I liked to draw flowers too. But they would not always turn out well. I could identify what type of flower they were but they looked like they should have been on a cartoon strip.

I remember while I was living in the Davis home. I got to experience a lot of First-like going to the dentist. Going through a lot of pain getting filling done for my rotted teeth.

My top front teeth were pretty crooked. The kids at school called my buck teeth.

I never did get braces. Every year, I had to have a school physical done, and the required shots. YUCK! YUCK! YUCK!

There were a lot of good things that made my heart swell with love and of course there were sad times too.

I remember learning to swim. My older foster sister Nedra took it upon herself to teach me to swim. She felt that this was a necessary life skill to have. I suffered a bad panic attack that day.

Nedra did not know that I had come close to drowning in my past. I felt that I owed her an explanation

Since she seen me at my worst.

After that, Nedra would not let me give into my fear, but she did take the lessons a lot slower. I became a passable swimmer. But even to this day, I will not get in water alone.

I am sure that she told Mom about my past..

Every Sunday, I would watch the Nuns at Mass. I was very impressed that for all intents and purposes they each made a lifetime commitment to be married to Jesus.

I wondered if I could fit into that kind of Life when I became an adult. I would often wonder where I would actually live and how would I survive after I turned 18.

I knew that I had Blood Relatives but no real family that cared about me. If they actually cared, then I would be with them and not living in the custody of the State. I guess in reality, you can't expect cousins to want to take on extra burdens that isn't their own.

I know growing up, I was in survival mode all the time. You always have to think of the future, since you had no safety net, like a loving family to run to in times of crisis.

My social worker explained to me that basically all she and her agency could do was to try to give me a bed and shelter until my 18th birthday, then it was ADIOS!

There was a lot of fun times while I was in the Davis Foster home. . My sister Sara tried teaching me to roller skate and Ice Skate. Hitting the hard ground and hard Ice was very painful. I carried so many bruises. I was in a lot of pain. I found out quick that I have no athletic skills at all. I'd rather spend my time reading a good adventure book. While I was in that home, my foster mother's sister Jessica got into a terrible car wreck. This event caused some major changes for everyone in our home.

CHAPTER 3

Aunt Jessica

The day that Mrs. Davis got the call about her sister Jessica was so sad. I started thinking about my own mother who did not survive her car wreck. I saw the family fall apart that day. Our happy home became very unhappy.

I had only met Jessica one time before. She was a very nice lady who liked to ride horses and barrel race. *Remember feeling jealous and hurt that I was robbed of my mother while their Aunt lived.*

Through the coming months, there was no more shopping days or any kind of celebrations in the home.

My foster mother, Mrs. Davis spent most of her time at the hospital with her sister Jessica. We were told that her car brakes had failed.

Jessica ended up having very bad scars all over her body. She also became paralyzed from the neck down. She had lost the ability to speak properly.

Many nights I could hear Sara and Nedra crying while in their beds. I never let them know that I heard them, because I understood tears.

Jessica stayed in the hospital for several months. The day that she was released, her parents moved in with her to take care of her daily needs.

There was no money for a private nurse.so it was up to Jessica's family to take care of her.

That is the one thing that I have always admired about Catholic Families. They tend to pull together in times of Crisis.

It was decided that Jessica would need more help than her aging parents could provide.

My foster parents had to go through a procedure that was required by the state, to be able to keep us foster children with them, because we had to move to a different town in order to live with Jessica.

That year, I know all of us went through some emotional changes. I had got too comfortable in my daily routine and had to move again to a totally different environment.

Moving meant starting over in a new school, church and a lot of different responsibilities.

Aunt Jessica could not speak clearly, so it was hard to understand her.

We came from the city to live in a rural area. Not only was the physical environment was different, so were the country people. Their lifestyles were so different than what we were used to.

The one thing that I really liked was the two horses. I used to watch Jessica when she would be outside

On nice weather days .She would watch the horses for what seemed like hours. I wish that I could have read her mind. I can only imagine the heartbreak that she was feeling. I bet that she wished that she could have shed that broken body and walked away. Being trapped in that body, not being able to even lift a single finger, to pet her beloved horses. I wonder if her mind replayed all the years of barrel racing and all the ribbons and prizes that she got.

There were times when she would try to talk to me. I would get nervous, because I could not understand her. There were times when she would drool on herself. At first, I got grossed out but I eventually got used to it.

Jessica and I became Friends. I used to feel sorry for myself. Being around Jessica taught me how self-centered I truly was. I had absolutely nothing to complain about. I took life for granted,

The very next breath that we take is not guaranteed to any of us. Jessica was living proof of that.

I believe that God has his Lessons for all of us, and Jessica was my lesson. I never got to help bath or dress Jessica, but I did get to feed her.

While we lived with Jessica, we no longer went to mass. It was too hard to try to get her in a car.

I often wonder if Jessica had raging anger inside of her like a volcano waiting to explode. If she did, I would not have blamed her. I wonder if she was angry with God for having her Life suddenly ripped

From her so brutally .She never displayed any type of anger on the outside.

I remember her lopsided smile and beautiful blue eyes. Her face was badly scared. But her eyes is what got aq person's attention.

While I was with Jessica, I would often think about what my Mom's life would have been like if she would have survived her car wreck. Would she be unable to physically function like Jessica.

How would she handle it emotionally? Being trapped in a useless body. I started being relieved that my mother was not suffering any more.

Being paralyzed brings its own health challenges. While we lived with Jessica, her health continued to deteriorate. She eventually passed away; the cause of death was a bacterial infection in her lungs.

I wonder if when she was in the Hospital for the last time, if she asked God to take her home.

No one knows for absolute certainty what happens after death. I hope that where ever Jessica is,

That she is having a wonderful time barrel racing and that her life if filled with Joy!!!

Ella Walker

To order additional copies of this book, contact:
Xlibris
1-888-795-4274
www.Xlibris.com
Orders@Xlibris.com

Printed in the United States
By Bookmasters